MW01625168
this book
belongs to:
love

HEY, KIDS, THIS BOOK IS FOR YOU!

Why do you need a book full of questions? Well, once you start, you'll see that it's quite fun. You'll discover things about yourself, and, if you're filling it out as a family, you'll all learn more about each other. You'll let your desires be known and you'll be able to express your feelings. Over the course of filling out this book, you'll see that you will become a really creative thinker, too.

1 Here's how to use this book: You can fill it out on your own as a personal journal. Or, you can fill it out with your family. It's fun to discuss the questions and learn about each other.

2 There are no wrong answers here. They're all correct; after all, this is about your point of view. You get to be you and say what you think and feel.

3 Rather schmooze than write? You can do that, too. These questions can also be used as fun discussion topics.

4 This book is also designed to be able to be filled out twice, one year after another. You can look back at the previous year, see what you thought then, and notice what you might think differently about now. You'll end up with lots of memories down on paper that you might not have remembered!

First Paperback Edition / First Impression — July 2022 / The Jewish Kids Journal

ISBN # 1-4226-3193-1 / 978-1-4226-3193-5

A week, a month, or a year from now:
What will you remember most about
TODAY?

תשׁ// 20

תשׁ// 20

20 // תש

20 // תש

Which FOOD TRADITION is your favorite (i.e., apple in honey, charoses, or something else)?

If you could know one thing
ABOUT YOUR FUTURE,
what would it be?

תש//20

תש//20

תש//20

תש//20

I help prepare for Shabbos by ________.

What have you done recently that you're PROUD OF?

תש//20

תש//20

Wow

DESCRIBE ONE TIME THAT YOU SAW **Hashem answer a tefillah** RIGHT AWAY.

תש//20

תש//20

What would life be like if
NO ONE HAD A PHONE?

What's your favorite fruit or vegetable?

What do you like about it?

WHAT ADVICE would you give a younger brother or sister?

תש//20

תש//20

תש // 20

תש // 20

WHAT IS ONE THING
most people don't know about you?

תש//20

If you could go **BACK IN TIME** and change something in your life, what would it be?

תש//20

תש//20

תש//20

WHICH THREE WORDS best describe Succos to you?

תש//20

תש//20

תש//20

תש//20

If you were given a blank sheet of paper, what would you do with it?

What do you like most about YOUR SUCCAH?

תש//20

תש//20

What's your EARLIEST MEMORY?

עבר

20//תש

20//תש

My favorite
YOM TOV/CHAG
is ______. Why?

20//תש

20//תש

Name three things you are THANKFUL FOR.

20//תש

20//תש

נודה

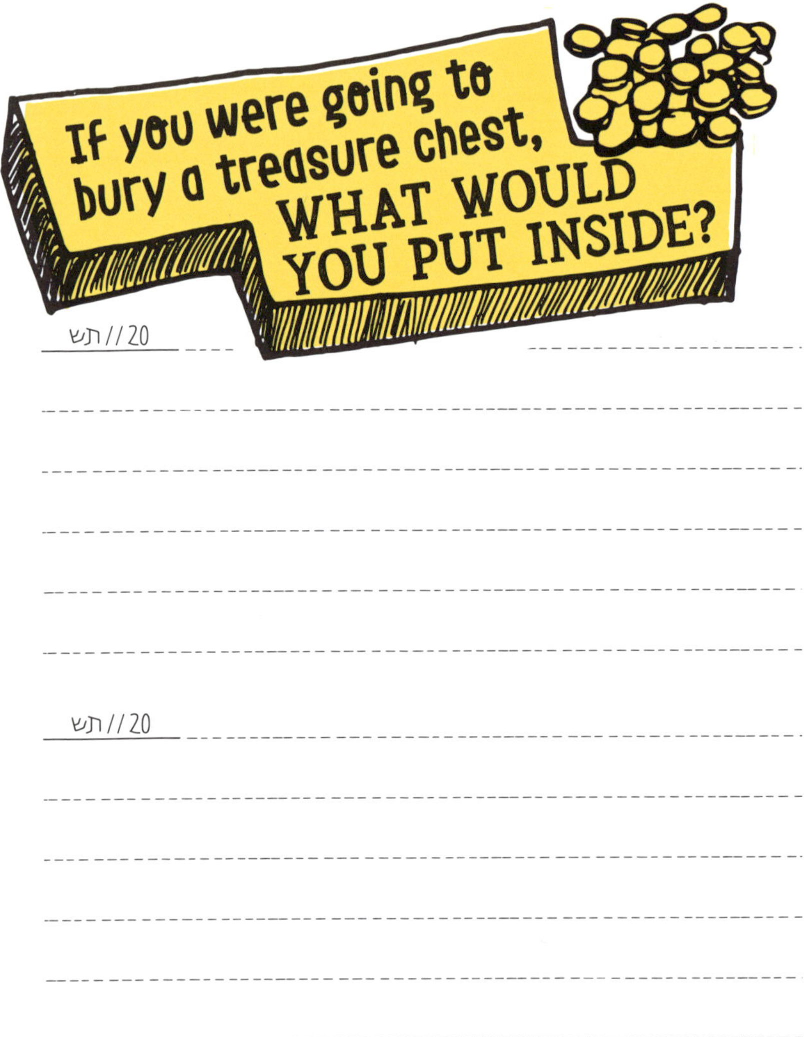
If you were going to
bury a treasure chest,
WHAT WOULD
YOU PUT INSIDE?
תש//20
תש//20

20//תש

20//תש

What was the best
Chol Hamoed trip you ever took?

20//תש

20//תש

תש//20

תש//20

I deserve a

GOLD MEDAL

in ____________.

If you could be Noach's helper on the teivah,

which animal would you want to take care of?

20//תש

20//תש

תש//20

תש//20

If you could design your school uniform,

WHAT WOULD IT LOOK LIKE?

If you could spend a day in the time of MOSHE RABBEINU OR DAVID HAMELECH, which would you choose?

20 // תש

20 // תש

I WISH I could _____ all day.

תש//20

תש//20

I'm a GOOD FRIEND because ______.

תשׁ // 20

תשׁ // 20

תש//20

תש//20

If you could cook or bake one dish by yourself, WHAT WOULD IT BE?

What's your favorite Shabbos party treat?
What's your second favorite?

תש//20

תש//20

תש//20

תש//20

What's one thing you'd NEVER CHANGE ABOUT YOURSELF?

תש//20

תש//20

What are some things that you LIKE TO SHARE?

תש//20

תש//20

If it raained for 40 days and 40 nights, I would ____.

__/__/20

__/__/20

תש//20

תש//20

What are your most and least favorite CHORES?

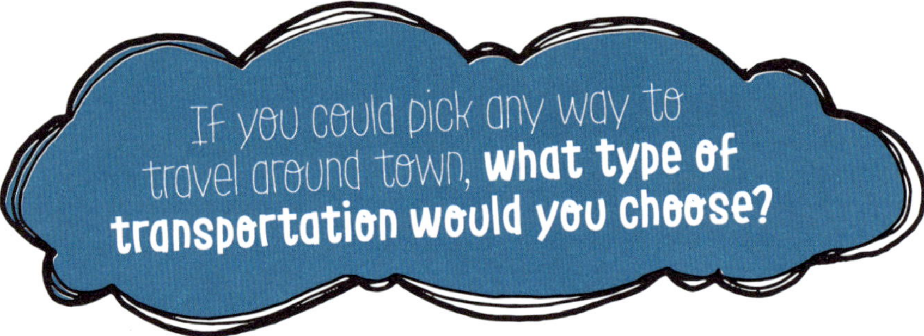
If you could pick any way to travel around town, **what type of transportation would you choose?**

תש// 20

תש// 20

תש//20

תש//20

What would you do if you were given A MILLION DOLLARS?

תש//20

תש//20

What is one thing you own that you would NEVER GIVE AWAY?

תש//20

תש//20

What makes YOU SPECIAL?

Do you have a FAVORITE PLACE in your town?

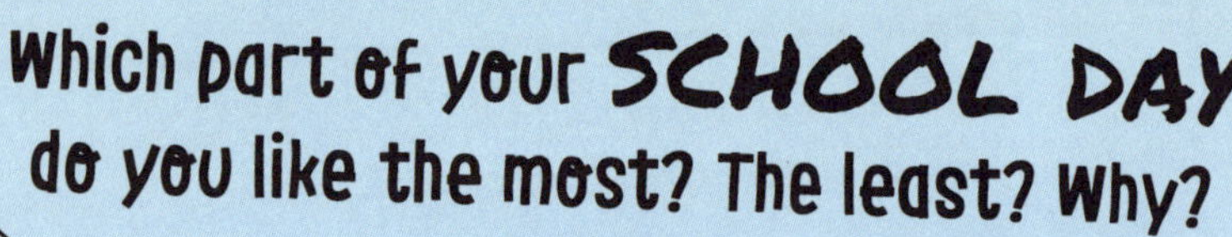
Which part of your SCHOOL DAY
do you like the most? The least? Why?

תש//20

תש//20

20//תש

20//תש

שלום

In how many languages
can you say "Hello"?

תש//20

תש//20

תש//20

תש//20

IF I WERE AN ARTIST,

I would paint a _______, because ________________.

You have $1 a day for tzedakah.
TO WHOM WOULD YOU GIVE IT?

20//תש

20//תש

צדקה

תש//20

תש//20

When you're waiting, **HOW DO YOU SPEND THE TIME?**

Someone who knows me well would DESCRIBE ME using these words: ____ and ______.

תש//20

תש//20

How long does it take you to **GET DRESSED IN THE MORNING?**

תש//20

תש//20

Who is your FAVORITE PERSON in Sefer Bereishis? Why?

תש//20

תש//20

You won a $1,000 GIFT CARD to one store of your choice. Which store would you choose?

20//תש

20//תש

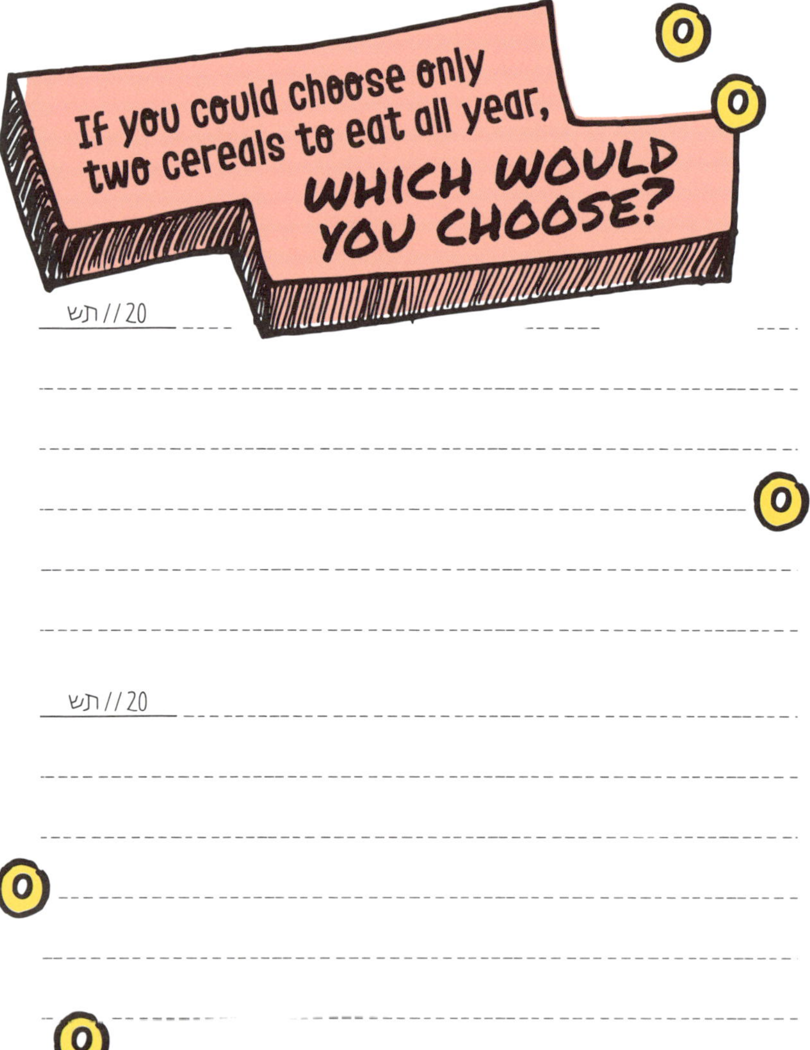
If you could choose only two cereals to eat all year,
WHICH WOULD YOU CHOOSE?

20//תש

20//תש

20 / / תש

20 / / תש

I appreciate it when I come **HOME FROM SCHOOL** and ______.

20// תש

YOU'RE BUYING A PRESENT. What are you buying? For whom are you buying it?

20// תש

20//תש

20//תש

How can you show grown-ups that you're RESPONSIBLE enough to ______?

What's your favorite game or activity to PLAY WITH YOUR FRIENDS?

תש//20

תש//20

20//תש

20//תש

What's one special thing that you CAN DO FOR A GUEST?

IF I COULD LEARN A NEW SKILL,
I would like to learn how to ______.

תש//20

תש//20

WHICH BOOK DO YOU READ
over and over and still love?

כסלו

תש//20

תש//20

Have you ever taught something to someone else? WHAT WAS IT?

תש// 20

תש// 20

תש // 20

תש // 20

What's your full Hebrew name?

What does it mean to you?

כסלו

IF YOU HAD A ROBOT, what would you ask it to do for you?

20//תש

20//תש

Describe a time when you were VERY BRAVE.

תש//20

תש//20

THIS COMING SHABBOS

I want to ________.

20//תש

20//תש

Who is your hero?
WHY?

כסלו

20//תש

20//תש

What type of donuts do you like best (what fillings and/or toppings)?

תש//20

תש//20

תש//20

תש//20

WHEN I'm going to sleep, I like ______.

כסלו

Z
z
z
z

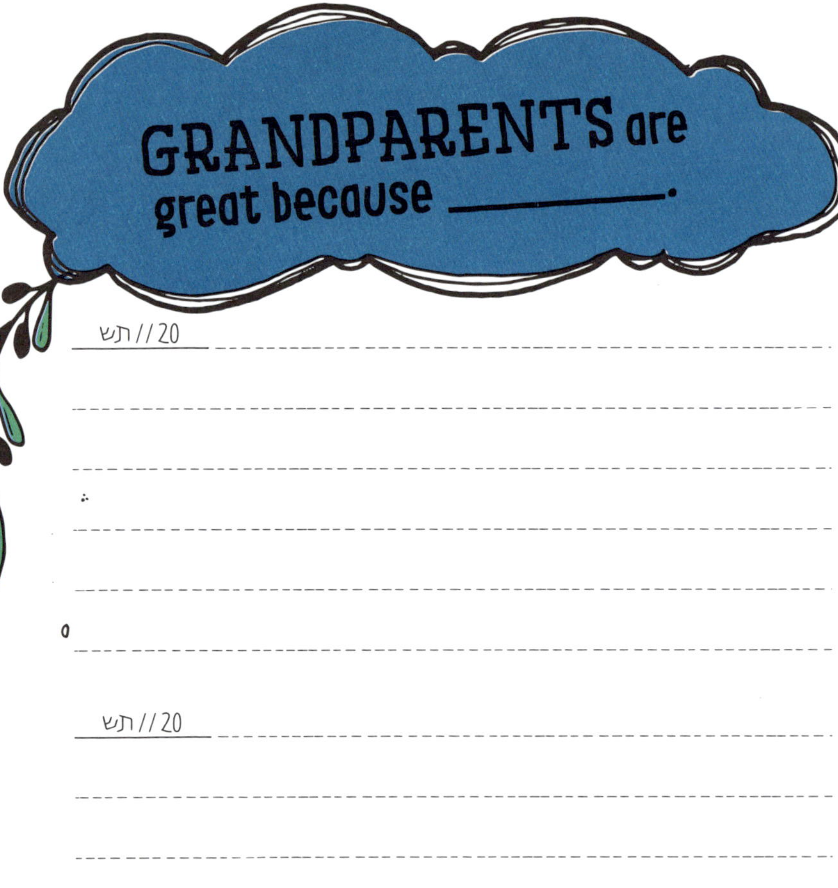

תש//20

תש//20

תש//20

תש//20

What's the STRANGEST FOOD you've ever eaten?

תש//20

תש//20

I LIKE IT WHEN MY FAMILY ______ together.

What's one CHANUKAH PRESENT you always wanted but never received?

What's your favorite CHANUKAH MEMORY?

תש//20

20//תש

20//תש

20//תש

20//תש

Who is your favorite COUSIN? Why?

תש//20

תש//20

If you could only keep ONE TOY, which one would it be?

20// תש

20// תש

שבת

What's the STRANGEST thing in your backpack?

WHICH MIRACLE in Jewish history would you most want to witness?

תש//20

תש//20

20//תש

20//תש

What's the SILLIEST DREAM you've ever had?

IF YOU COULD ADD ONE ROOM TO YOUR HOUSE, **what kind of room would it be?**

תש//20

תש//20

If you could speak to a Holocaust survivor, WHICH QUESTIONS WOULD YOU ASK?

תש//20

תש//20

What's your
FAVORITE ROOM
or spot in the house?

תשׁ//20

תשׁ//20

Do you like it better when the weather is warm and raining, or when it's cold and snowing?

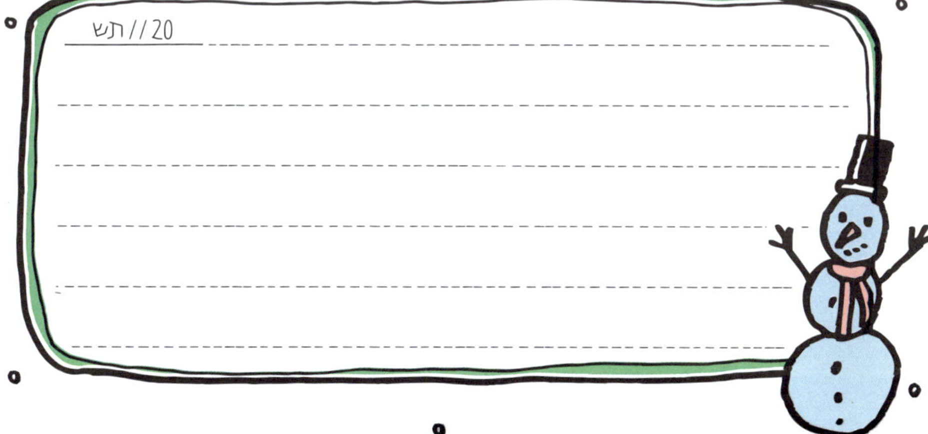

If you could take one day off from school, WHAT WOULD YOU WANT TO DO?

תש// 20

תש// 20

תש//20

תש//20

What SUPERHUMAN POWER do you wish you had?

20// תש

20// תש

When do you feel COZY AND CALM?

20//תש

20//תש

What are you ESPECIALLY GOOD AT?

What is the best thing ABOUT BEING A KID?

20 // תש

20 // תש

20//תש

20//תש

If you could switch seats with anyone in class,

WHO WOULD IT BE? WHY?

What's better for dinner:
DAIRY OR MEAT?

WHICH INSTRUMENT
do you wish you could play? Why?

סתיו

20//תש

20//תש

IN MY FAMILY, I am the ______.

תש//20

תש//20

20//תש

20//תש

Which would you rather have in your home:

a giant ballpit or a slide instead of a staircase?

If you had to eat the same meal everyday, WHAT WOULD IT BE?

תש//20

תש//20

תש//20

תש//20

MY FAMILY is especially careful with ______.

___ /___ /20תש

___ /___ /20תש

Describe something that's **BLACK AND WHITE.**

תש//20

תש//20

Which possession that was BROKEN OR LOST do you miss?

תש//20

תש//20

תש//20

תש//20

What's your favorite
RECESS ACTIVITY?

תש//20

תש//20

תש//20

תש//20

What's the
BEST FAMILY TRIP
you ever took?

What's the best part
of a SNOW DAY?
תש//20
תש//20

IF YOU WERE THE PRESIDENT,
what law would you make or change?

YOU FORGOT TO DO YOUR HOMEWORK.
What happens next?

WHAT'S THE FIRST THING YOU THOUGHT ABOUT **when you woke up this morning?**

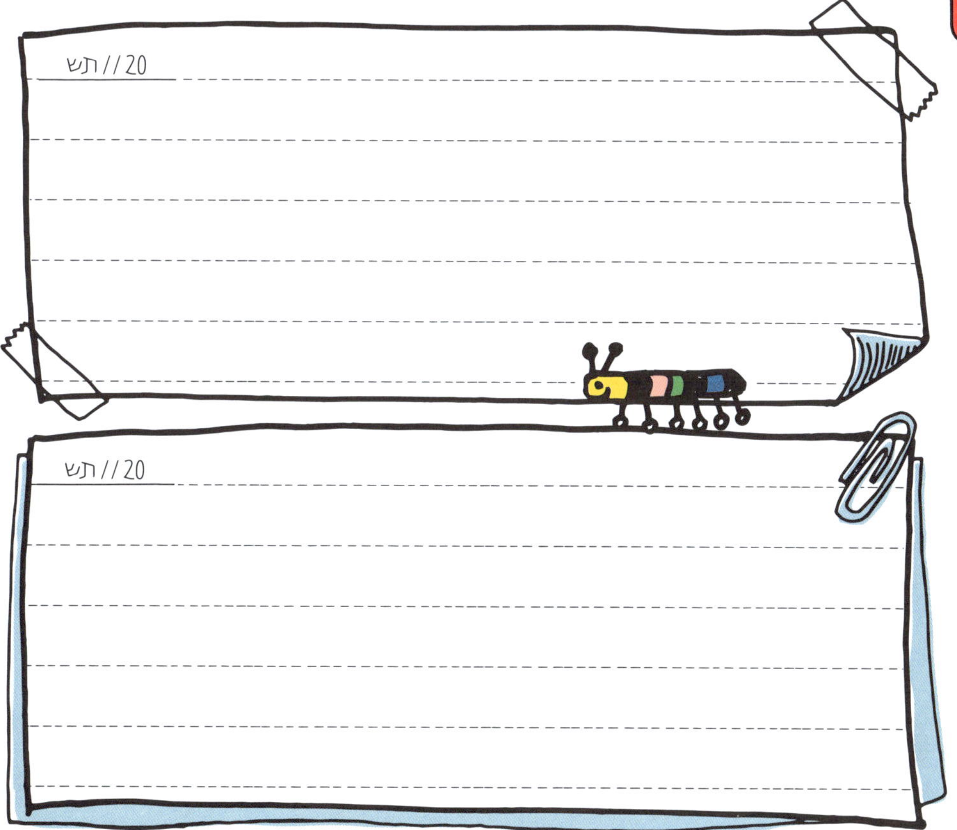

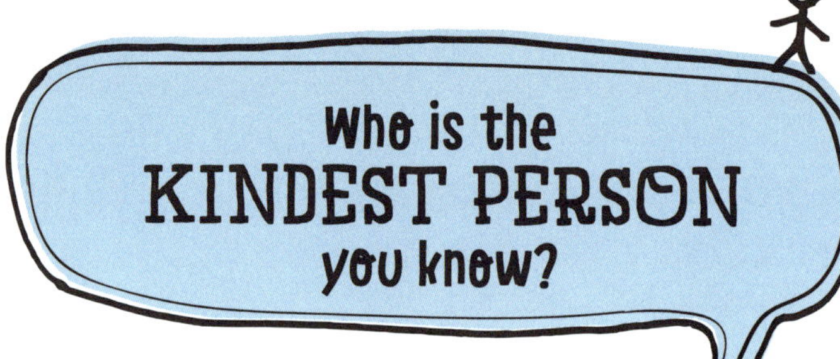

תש//20

תש//20

20//תש

20//תש

What's your FAVORITE THING to do when you are alone?

20//תש

20//תש

What is one thing you wish YOU COULD DO NOW instead of waiting until you are older?

תש//20

תש//20

What's your favorite kind of CHOCOLATE?

I COMPLAIN the most about ________.

תש//20

תש//20

20//תש

20//תש

Where is one place

YOU'LL NEVER GO?

Would you rather be the BEST PLAYER on a losing team or the WORST PLAYER on a winning team?

תש//20

תש//20

What's your favorite sandwich?

(Name the type of bread and the fillings.)

תש//20

תש//20

Would you rather be able to SPEAK EVERY LANGUAGE in the world or PLAY EVERY INSTRUMENT?

תש//20

תש//20

Which of the SHIVAH MINIM is your favorite?

תש // 20

תש // 20

תש//20

תש//20

תש//20

תש//20

WHAT DO YOU WISH you had more time to do?

20// תש

What do you LIKE BEST about the city/ town you live in?

20// תש

תש// 20

תש// 20

Would you rather visit
the BEIS HAMIKDASH
or walk through
KRIYAS YAM SUF?

WHAT'S YOUR FAVORITE SNACK?
Where do you most like to enjoy it?
תש//20
תש//20

20//תש

20//תש

IF YOU ARE LOOKING FOR ME,

you can always find me at______.

What's one of your **TALENTS?**

תש//20

תש//20

What is your favorite TIME OF THE DAY? Why?

20//תש

20//תש

HAPPY

What sound makes you feel FRIGHTENED?

תשׁ // 20

תשׁ // 20

20//תש

20//תש

IF YOU WERE A FAMOUS PERSON,

what would you be famous for?

WHAT'S YOUR FAVORITE
board or card game?
2
6
1
3
20// תש
20// תש

20//תש

20//תש

What's your favorite PART OF SHABBOS?

_____ /ת/// 20ש

_____ /ת/// 20ש

Tell a JOKE.

תש//20

תש//20

The best SONG TO DANCE TO is ______.

תש//20

תש//20

תש//20

תש//20

What's one of the most amazing things HASHEM CREATED?

תש//20

תש//20

תש//20

תש//20

What are three words you would use to describe **YOUR NEIGHBORHOOD?**

YOU'RE GOING AWAY FOR SHABBOS

and you're packing your ______.

___/___/20 תש

___/___/20 תש

If you could travel to any time in the past, which time would you visit? Why?

תש // 20

תש // 20

What's one thing YOU'LL NEVER DO?

תשע//20

תשע//20

If you could open a store, WHAT WOULD YOU SELL THERE?

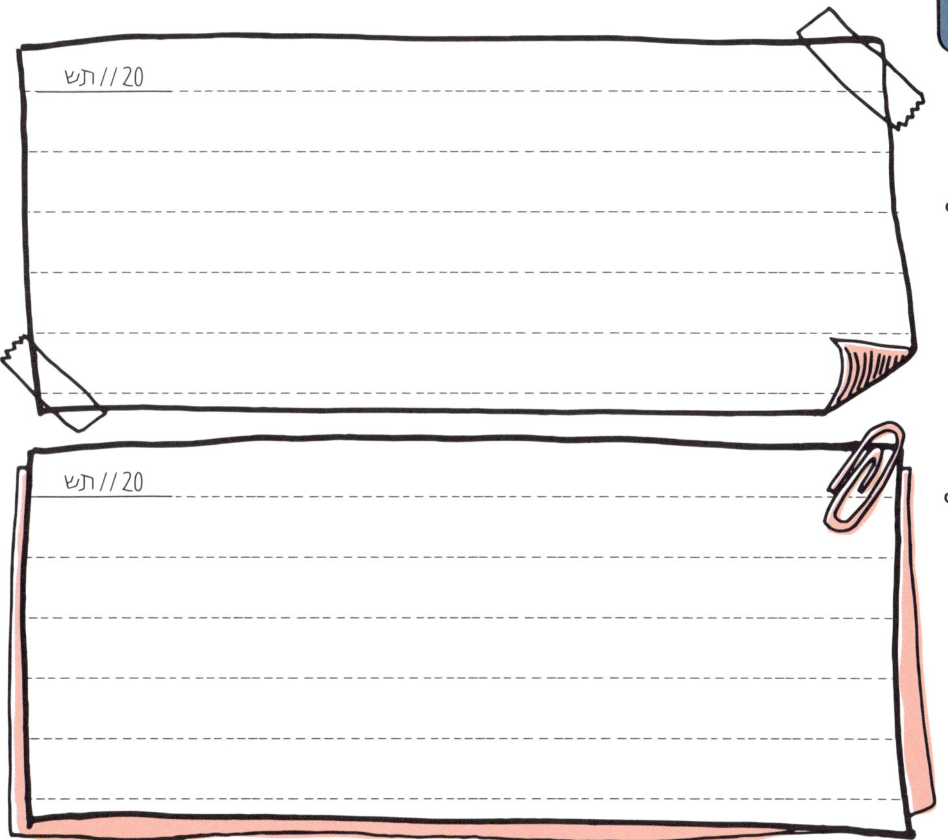

I DON'T LIKE to be told to ____.

תש//20

תש//20

תש//20

תש//20

What was your favorite
PURIM COSTUME?

20//תש

20//תש

If you could talk to any person in MEGILLAS ESTHER, who would it be?

20//תש

20//תש

What was the **FUNNIEST PURIM COSTUME** you ever saw?

If you had three wishes, WHAT WOULD THEY BE?

20 // תש

1

20 // תש

2

2

1

3

תש//20

תש//20

I would **LOVE TO LEARN** how to ________.

WHAT MAKES YOU FEEL BETTER
when you don't feel well?

תש//20

תש//20

IF YOU COULD MAKE UP A NEW SCHOOL SUBJECT, what would it be?

תש//20

תש//20

If you had a chance to eat DESSERT FOR BREAKFAST every day, what would you choose?

תש//20

תש//20

I REMEMBER

the first time I tried to ________.

תש//20

תש//20

If your friend is sad,
what would you do to
make him/her feel better?
תש//20
תש//20

תש//20

תש//20

תש//20

תש//20

תש//20

תש//20

LOOK
Where's the best place to hide during a game of
HIDE AND SEEK?
תש//20
תש//20

תש//20

תש//20

yummy

You're asked to prepare dinner and you're sent to the store with $12 to buy ingredients.

WHAT'S FOR DINNER?

When was the last time you wanted to say, "I QUIT"? Did you?

תשׁ// 20

תשׁ// 20

WHAT TOY HAVE YOU OUTGROWN that you used to love?

תש//20

תש//20

What is your favorite thing about having SIBLINGS/COUSINS?

תש // 20

תש // 20

תש//20

תש//20

When I become a bar/bas mitzvah, I will ________.

(Or, Since my bar/bas mitzvah, I have ______)

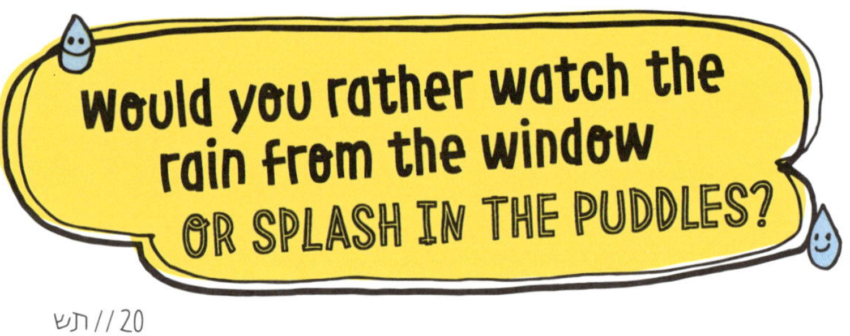
Would you rather watch the
rain from the window
OR SPLASH IN THE PUDDLES?

תש//20

תש//20

What would you like to accomplish before your
NEXT BIRTHDAY?

תש//20

תש//20

Give yourself a COMPLIMENT.

תש//20

תש//20

Can you DESCRIBE A COLOR without naming it?

תש//20

תש//20

WHEN I'M OLDER,

I want to be known as ____________.

תש//20

תש//20

תש//20

תש//20

My HOBBY is ________.

תש//20

תש//20

20//תש

20//תש

Which THREE WORDS would you use to describe Pesach?

What's your favorite part of THE SEDER?

תש//20

תש//20

Answer the following question with a question:

What makes this book different from other books?

ניסן

תש// 20

תש// 20

What would you grab if MASHIACH CAME RIGHT NOW?

WHICH FOOD IS BETTER
on Pesach than all year round?

20//תש

20//תש

תש//20

תש//20

תש//20

תש//20

If you could name your future kids,
WHAT NAMES WOULD YOU CHOOSE?

תש//20

If you could watch one of the **MAKKOS** (from a safe spot in Goshen), which would you like to see?

תש//20

תש//20

תש//20

What's **ONE THING** that is important to your parents?

What do you like more: being indoors or outdoors? Why?

תש//20

תש//20

תש//20

תש//20

WHEN PEOPLE COME TO YOU FOR HELP,
what do they usually want you to do?

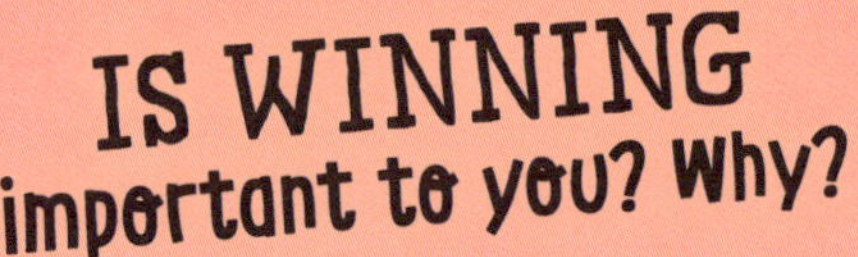

IS WINNING important to you? Why?

תשע//20

תשע//20

What topping do you LIKE BEST ON CHALLAH?

תש//20

תש//20

If you could instantly become an EXPERT IN ANY SUBJECT, which would you choose? Why?

תש//20

תש//20

How would you spend 24 HOURS in Eretz Yisrael?

20//תש

20//תש

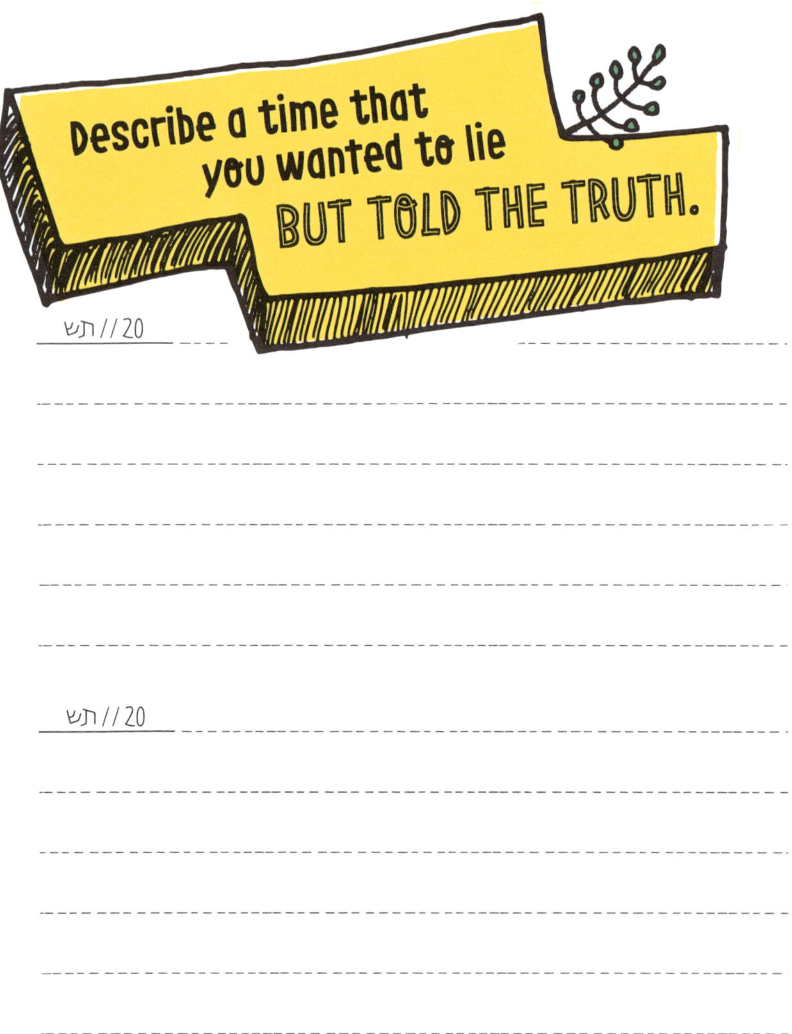
Describe a time that you wanted to lie
BUT TOLD THE TRUTH.
תש//20
תש//20

תש//20

תש//20

What's your FAVORITE SPORT? Why?

תש//20

What's ONE THING grownups help you with...but you think you can do by yourself?

תש//20

תש//20

תש//20

Who is your FAVORITE fictional character?

תש//20

תש//20

תשׁ//20

תשׁ//20

Would you rather have the ability to

BE INVISIBLE OR TO FLY?

What kind of person do you think you WANT TO MARRY?

תש// 20

תש// 20

It's HARD FOR ME to

______________.

תשׁ//20

תשׁ//20

What do you do to stay
STRONG AND HEALTHY?
תשׁ // 20
תשׁ // 20

תש//20

תש//20

Name two ideas to give someone who says, "I'M BORED."

What job or business would
you like to have
WHEN YOU'RE AN ADULT?

תש//20

תש//20

How much do you think these things cost?
1) A HOUSE 2) A CHALLAH
3) A PAIR OF SHOES

תש//20

תש//20

What's your favorite SHABBOS DESSERT?

20//תש

20//תש

Which other LANGUAGE would you love to know? Why?

תש // 20

תש // 20

If you had a ball of clay, WHAT WOULD YOU MOLD?

תש//20

תש//20

תש//20

תש//20

What's your favorite **JEWISH SONG?**

What's one way you can
TREAT OTHER PEOPLE
like you treat yourself?

תש // 20

תש // 20

תש//20

תש//20

When the WEATHER IS NICE, I ________.

תש//20

תש//20

What's the MOST IMPORTANT THING you've ever davened for?

20 // תש

20 // תש

If you could spend all day with **ONE PERSON**, who would it be? Why?

What would you tell THE FUTURE YOU?

תש//20

תש//20

What's your favorite **SUBJECT IN SCHOOL** (must choose one!)? Why?

תש//20

תש//20

20//תש

20//תש

WHEN I WAKE UP,

I ______.

סיוון

20// תש

20// תש

If you could pick one DAIRY FOOD to enjoy this Shavuos, what would it be?

תש//20

תש//20

סיון

You missed the bus.

WHAT HAPPENS NEXT?

What would you want your mahn (manna) TO TASTE LIKE?

תש//20

תש//20

20//תש

20//תש

What's something you can do to show

KAVOD HATORAH?

If you could ask someone in Megillas Rus a question, WHAT WOULD IT BE? WHY?

?

20//תש

20//תש

What three words describe what it means to be **A GOOD JEW?**

תש//20

תש//20

What time is YOUR BEDTIME? What time do you really fall asleep?

תש//20

WHERE'S THE FARTHEST

you can go from home by yourself and still know how to find your way back?

תש// 20

תש// 20

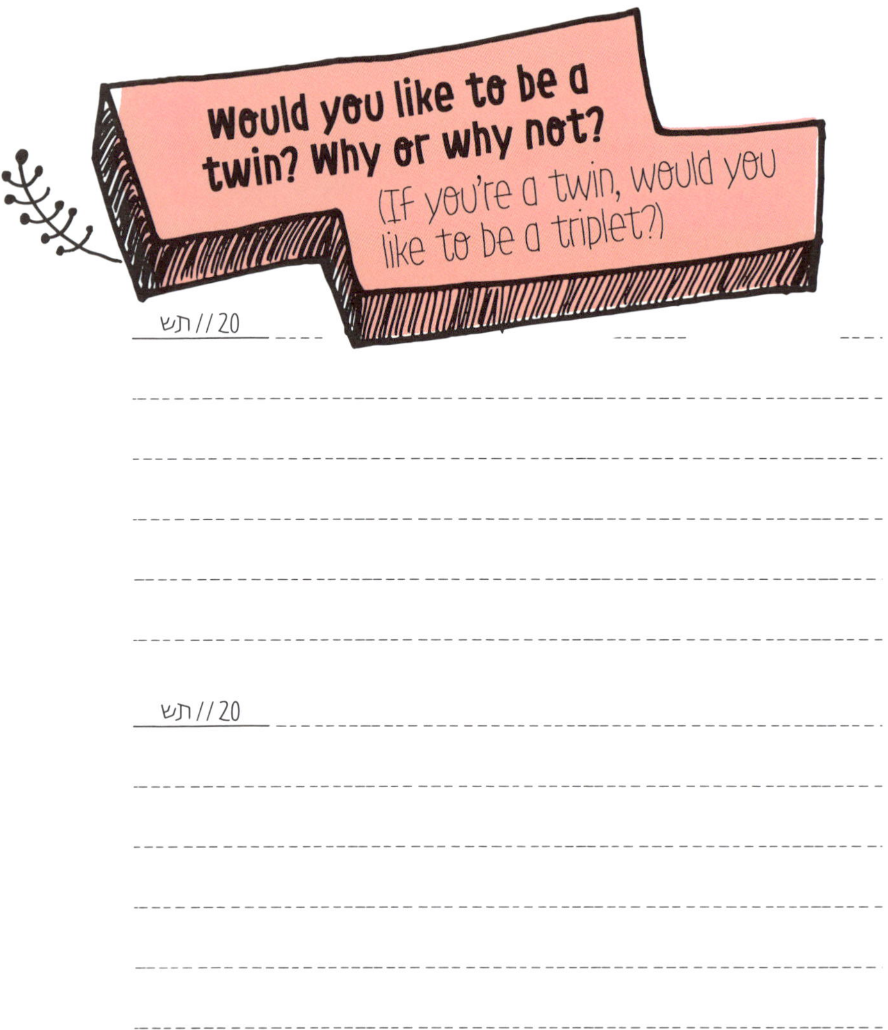
Would you like to be a twin? Why or why not?
(If you're a twin, would you like to be a triplet?)
תש // 20
תש // 20

תש//20

תש//20

Jun

Fun

What's **ONE FUN THING** everyone should try at least once? Why?

תש//20

תש//20

How can you cheer yourself up WHEN YOU ARE SAD?

happy

תש//20

תש//20

סיון

If you were a teacher,

WHICH SUBJECT WOULD YOU TEACH?

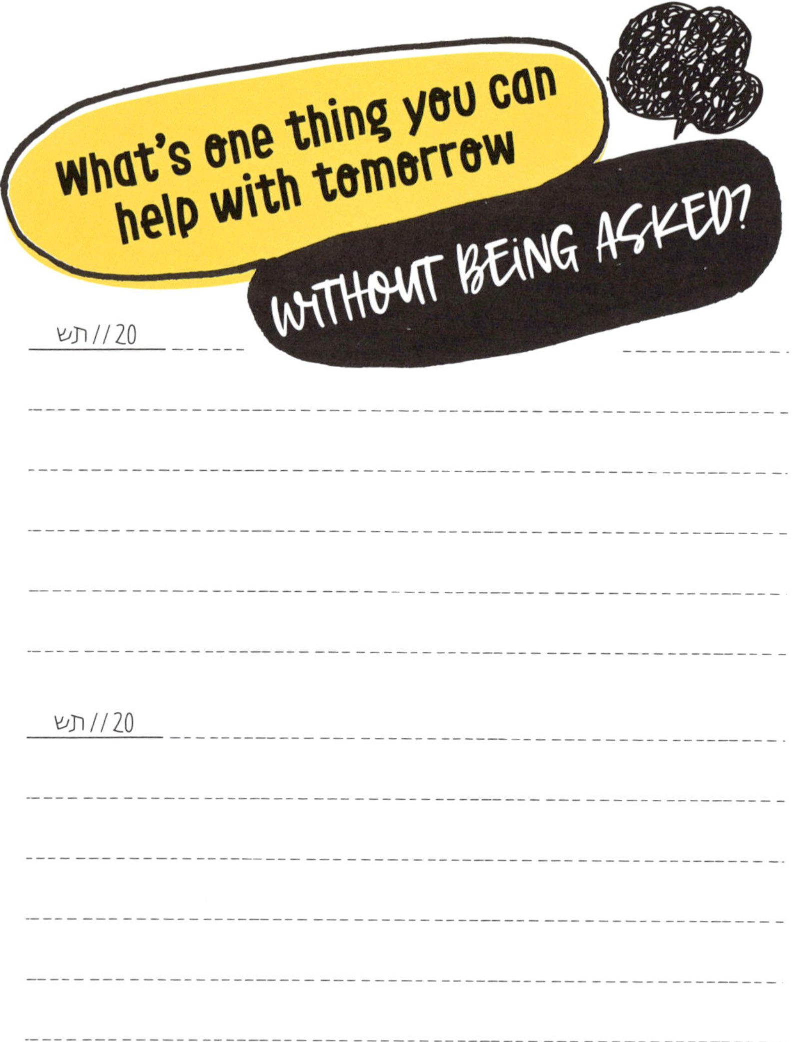
What's one thing you can help with tomorrow
WITHOUT BEING ASKED?
תש//20
תש//20

תש//20

תש//20

We're out of milk. Would you rather have cereal with

WATER, JUICE, OR SODA?

WOULD YOU RATHER HAVE
a flying car or a personal robot?

hello

תש//20

תש//20

Which PLANT OR FLOWER is your favorite? Why?

תש//20

תש//20

I would like to SAVE UP MONEY
to buy a ________.
תש//20
תש//20

תש//20

תש//20

Where do you think you'll live 20 YEARS FROM NOW?

WHAT'S THE MOST ANNOYING QUESTION
people always ask you?
תש//20
תש//20

WHAT'S UNIQUE ABOUT YOUR FAMILY
that makes you really proud?
20//תש
20//תש

What are you LOOKING FORWARD TO?

תש // 20

תש // 20

20//תש

20//תש

What's your FAVORITE BREAKFAST?

20//תש

20//תש

תש//20

תש//20

Who was your FAVORITE TEACHER?

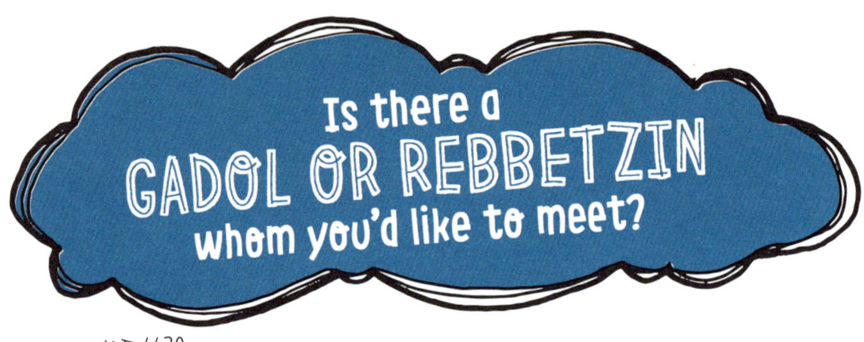

________ //20 תש

________ //20 תש

20//תש

20//תש

Would you rather: **Listen or speak? Read a book or hear a story? Draw or write?**

THIS SUMMER,
I want to ______.

תש//20

תש//20

What's the ULTIMATE COMPLIMENT your teacher could give you?

20//תש

20//תש

What's the BEST GIFT you've ever received?

תשׁ // 20

תשׁ // 20

What is one thing you REFUSE TO SHARE?

WHICH FOOD reminds
you of your family? Why?
תש//20
תש//20

תש//20

תש//20

ON A SCALE OF 1 TO 10,
______ is a 10.

20 // תש

20 // תש

When I'm a MOTHER/FATHER, I will ____.

תש // 20

תש // 20

תמוז

What is your favorite WORD?

?

Everyone thinks it's *funny* when I ________.

תש//20

תש//20

תש//20

תש//20

What's one CANDY you don't like?

IF YOU COULD HAVE A PEt,
which animal would you choose? Why?

תש//20

תש//20

What's your favorite thing to do OUTDOORS?

תש//20

תש//20

WHICH MITZVAH is most challenging to you? Why?

תש // 20

תש // 20

How do your grandparents make you FEEL LOVED?

תש//20

תש//20

To whom would you go if you needed help?
WHAT WOULD THAT PERSON HELP YOU DO?
תש//20
תש//20

תש//20

תש//20

Would you rather go to the **DOCTOR** or the **DENTIST?**

20//תש

20//תש

What's the first thing that comes to your mind:

I don't have to ______.

Shoes are ______.

It's easy to ______.

תשׁ// 20

תשׁ// 20

תמוז

Have you ever memorized anything?

WHAT WAS IT?

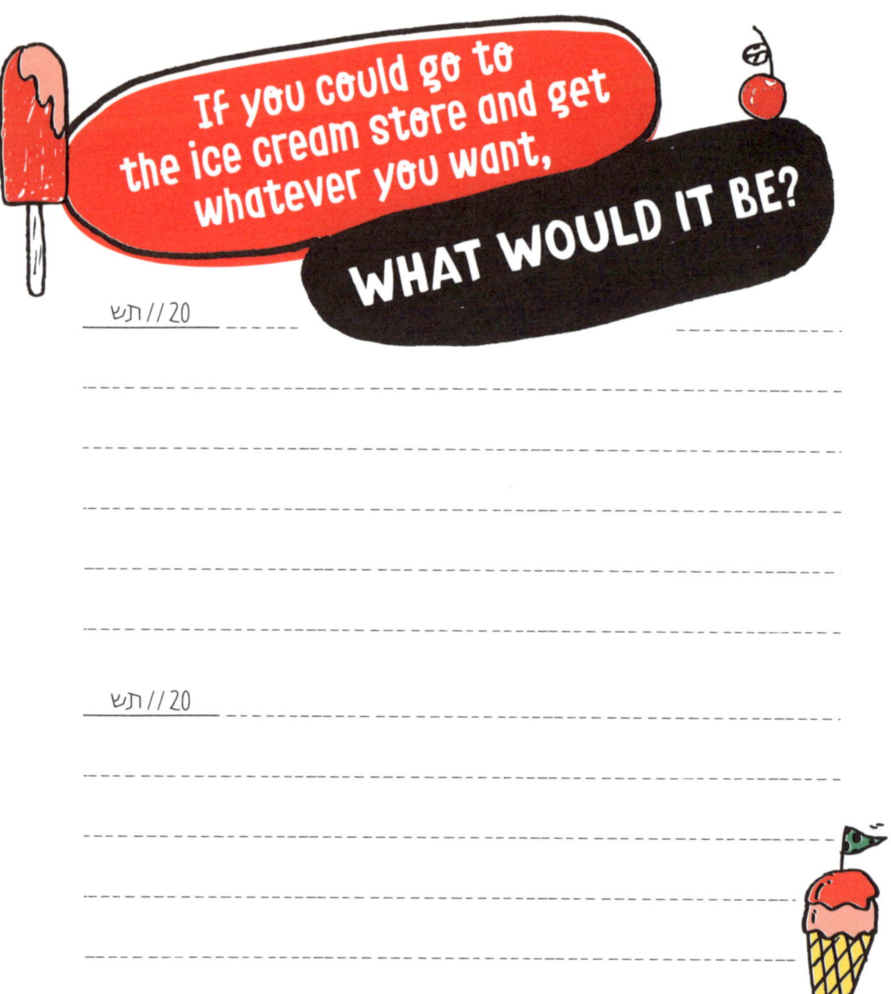
If you could go to the ice cream store and get whatever you want,
WHAT WOULD IT BE?

תש//20

תש//20

20 //תש

20 //תש

If you could start any chesed organization,

WHAT WOULD IT DO?

Would you rather play in the SNOW or the SPRINKLERS?

20//תש

20//תש

I like CHOLENT and ______.

תמוז

20 // תש

20 // תש

What's your favorite CAMP ACTIVITY?

תש//20

תש//20

תש//20

תש//20

What's one thing you'll be sure to do WHEN YOU'RE A PARENT?

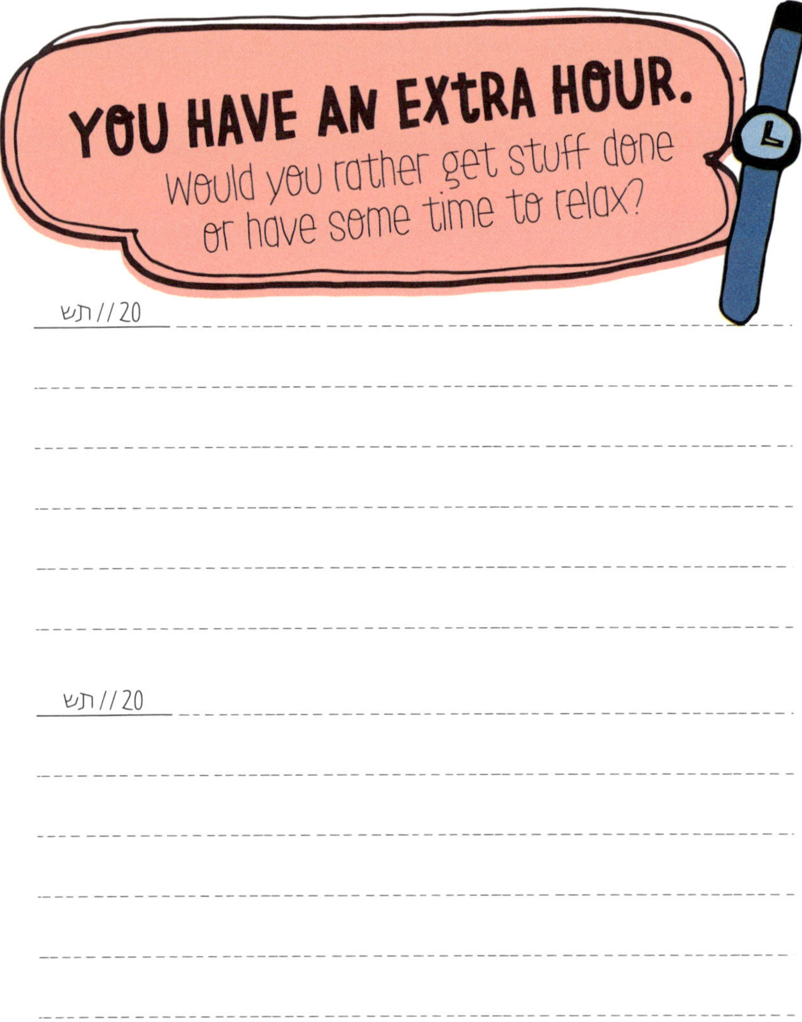
YOU HAVE AN EXTRA HOUR.
Would you rather get stuff done or have some time to relax?
תש//20
תש//20

If you could make any pizza, **WHAT WOULD BE ON IT?**

20//תש

20//תש

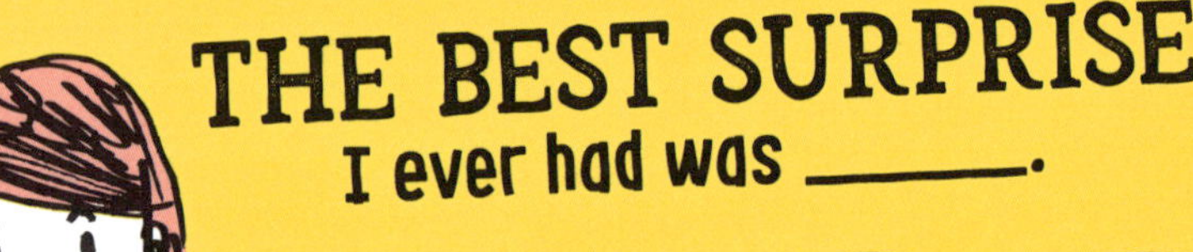

תש//20

תש//20

HASHEM is proud of me because ______.

20 // תש

20 // תש

What do you think adults forget about being A CHILD?

תשׁ//20

תשׁ//20

HEY

תש//20

תש//20

WHAT'S the oldest thing you've ever seen?

20//תש

20//תש

תש//20

תש//20

What comes to mind when you think of MOTZA'EI SHABBOS?

תש//20

תש//20

What takes up TOO MUCH OF YOUR TIME?

What's your favorite thing to do WHILE RIDING IN THE CAR?

If you were invisible for a day, WHAT WOULD YOU DO?

Is there any EXPRESSION OR PHRASE you say often?

תש // 20

תש // 20

20//תש

20//תש

What's a small thing that
MAKES YOUR
DAY BETTER?

תש//20

Whom do you like TO TALK TO ON THE PHONE?

תש//20

20 //תש

20 //תש

A siyum (or party) is held in your honor.

WHAT'S ON THE TABLE?

YOU'RE PAINTING YOUR ROOM.

What color would you choose?

ש//20תש

ש//20תש

תש//20

תש//20

IF YOU MADE AN INVENTION, what would it be?

What's the MOST USEFUL THING you own?

/ /20 תש

/ /20 תש

What's your **FAVORITE SMELL?**

תש//20

תש//20

Where is the most BEAUTIFUL PLACE you've ever been?

תש//20

תש//20

Describe the perfect **SUMMER DAY.**

תש//20

IF YOU WERE AN AUTHOR,
what would your book
be about?
תש//20
תש//20

20//תש

20//תש

Who would be your #1 GUEST to invite for Shabbos?

תש//20

תש//20

תש//20

תש//20

If you could be any age, **HOW OLD WOULD YOU BE?** Why?

If you could travel to any location,
WHERE WOULD YOU WANT TO GO?
תש//20
תש//20

20//תש

20//תש

If you had to trade places with someone for one day,

WHO WOULD IT BE?

What's your favorite TAKEOUT FOOD?

תש//20

תש//20

WHAT'S THE FARTHEST you've ever been from home?

20//תש

20//תש

I WISH I could always be as happy as ______.

תש//20

תש//20

תש//20

תש//20

What is your favorite day of the week

(ASIDE FROM SHABBOS)?

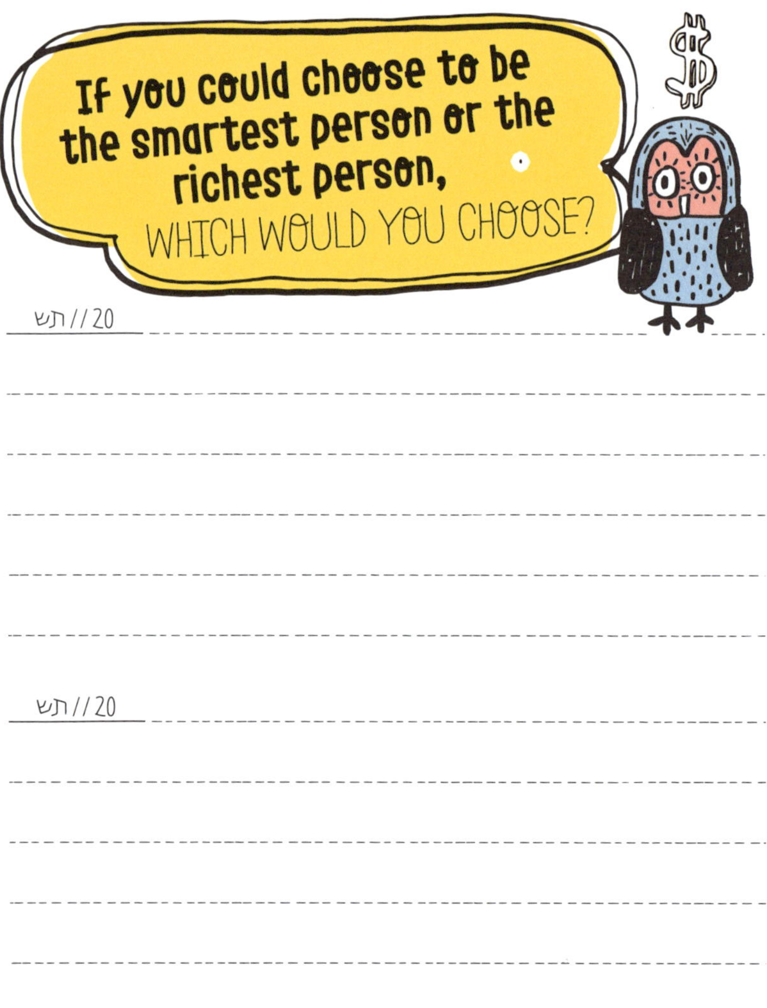
If you could choose to be the smartest person or the richest person,
WHICH WOULD YOU CHOOSE?
$

תש // 20

תש // 20

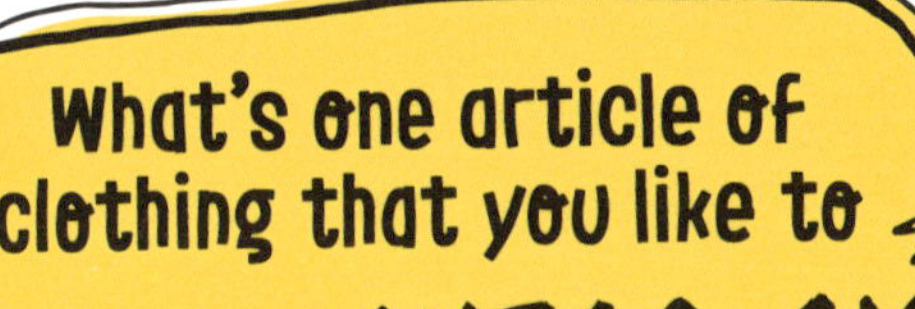

What's one article of clothing that you like to WEAR OVER AND OVER?

תש//20

תש//20

WHEN I HEAR A BABY CRY,
it makes me ______.

תש// 20

תש// 20

A BLESSING I have that I can share with others is ______.

20//תש

20//תש

I LOVE ____ more than ____.
תש//20
תש//20

תש//20

תש//20

What do you like least about GOING TO BED?

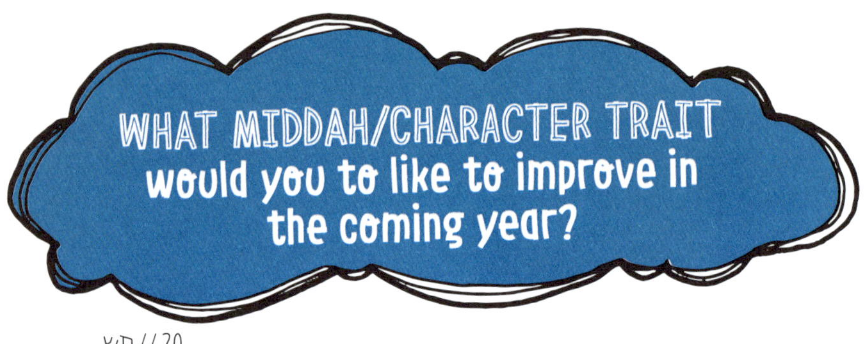
WHAT MIDDAH/CHARACTER TRAIT
would you to like to improve in
the coming year?

תש//20

תש//20

תש//20

תש//20

WHAT JOB
do you think is the best? Why?

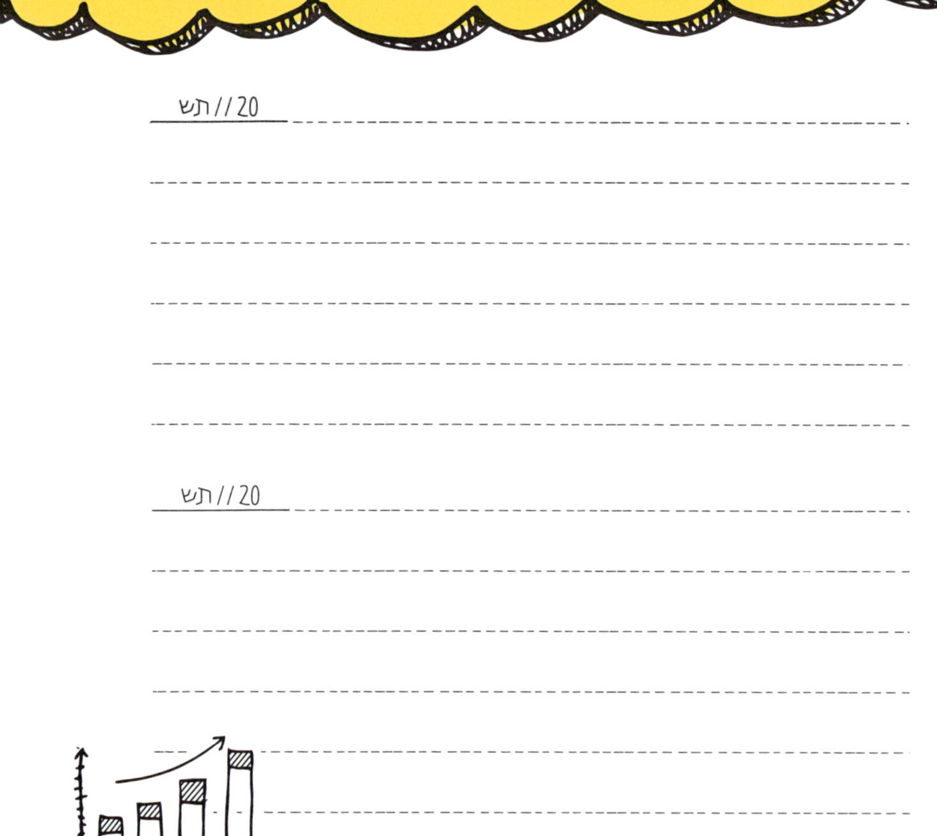

What's your **FAVORITE** time of day?

אלול

תש//20

תש//20

If you could ask Hashem one question,

WHAT WOULD IT BE?

What do you FIND SCARY?

תש//20

תש//20

WHAT'S THE YUMMIEST THING

that's She'hakol? Ha'adamah? Ha'etz? Mezonos?

תש//20

תש//20

תש//20

תש//20

If someone gave you $50 to spend today, WHAT WOULD YOU DO WITH IT?

20// תש

20// תש

HOW would you react if a bee was following you?

תש//20

תש//20

תש//20

תש//20

תש//20

תש//20

I didn't EXPECT ________.

THIS COMING SCHOOL YEAR,
I want to ____.

תש//20

תש//20

What do you want for dinner

ON YOUR BIRTHDAY?

Bonus

תש//20

תש//20

What do you ADMIRE MOST about one of your friends?

20 // תש

20 // תש

If you were an adult for a day, WHAT WOULD YOU DO?

תש//20

תש//20

WOULD YOU RATHER BE ABLE TO READ PEOPLE'S MINDS or know the location of every lost item?

תשׁ // 20

תשׁ // 20

20//תש

20//תש

20//תש

What's the **MOST USEFUL THING** you've learned?

20//תש

תש//20

תש//20

Bonus

How do you like YOUR EGGS?

If you could only pack four items in your suitcase,
WHAT WOULD THEY BE?
תש//20
תש//20

תש//20

תש//20

hi

_____ is a great way to make

NEW FRIENDS

How long do you spend DOING HOMEWORK?

תש//20

תש//20

IF YOU HAD A PARROT,
what would you teach it to say?

Bonus

20//תש

20//תש

I can make TOMORROW great by ______.
תש// 20
תש// 20

תש//20

תש//20

GIVE YOUR DAY A RATING: 1 TO 10.

Why did you choose that number?

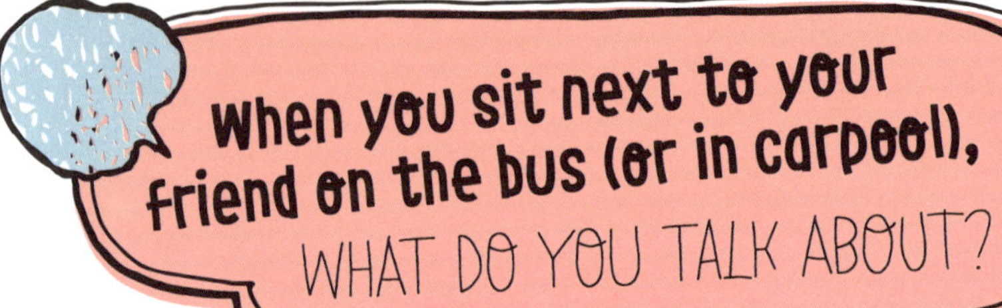
When you sit next to your friend on the bus (or in carpool),
WHAT DO YOU TALK ABOUT?

תש//20

תש//20

20//תש

20//תש

What do you think is a very DIFFICULT JOB? Why?

תשׁ//20

תשׁ//20

Do you like or dislike surprises?
WHY OR WHY NOT?

20 // תשׁ

20 // תשׁ

תש//20

תש//20

תש // 20

תש // 20

I felt JOYFUL today when ________.

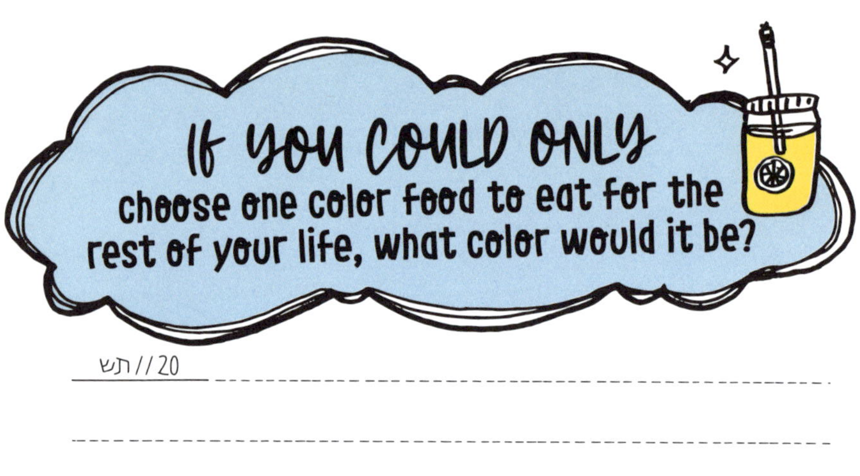
If you could only
choose one color food to eat for the rest of your life, what color would it be?

תשׁ//20

תשׁ//20

תשׁ // 20

תשׁ // 20

If you could erase one thing from the world,
WHAT WOULD IT BE?

If you could add a question to this book, WHAT WOULD IT BE?

20__ // __

20__ // __

Thank you to **all our kids** who are our best critics! You helped us decide which questions deserve to be in this book and which should be left out.

Thank you to **Rabbi Gedaliah Zlotowitz, Ahron Zlotowitz, Felice Eisner, Miriam Zakon, Chaya Felsinger,** and the **ArtScroll team** for our great continued partnership. Thank you, **Rachel Adler,** for always bringing our projects up a level.

Thank you **Fraidy Broker, Mati Iskowitz, Miriam Kohn, Miriam Yehudis Maryl, Goldy Seigfried,** and **Melinda Strauss** for your feedback and ideas.

Victoria Dwek,
Shaindy Menzer,
Renee Muller,
Leah Schapira,
Esti Waldman

Glossary

Beis HaMikdash — the Holy Temple in Yerushalayim.

bar mitzvah — 1. 13-year-old boy. 2. ceremony marking the coming of age of a Jewish boy.

bas mitzvah, bat mitzvah — 1. 12-year-old girl. 2. ceremony marking the coming of age of a Jewish girl.

chag (pl. **chagim**) — a holiday; a Jewish Festival.

challah (pl. **challos**) — loaves of soft wheat-bread traditionally eaten at a Shabbos meal.

Chanukah — Hanukah.

charoses—a dip usually made of chopped apples, nuts, and wine, used at the Passover Seder.

chesed — acts of kindness.

chol hamo'ed — the intermediate days between the first and last days of Pesach and of Succos.

cholent — (Yiddish) a stew prepared before Shabbos, simmered overnight, and traditionally eaten at Shabbos day meal.

David Hamelech — King David.

gadol (pl. **gedolim**) — literally, **great**; an outstanding Torah personality; a great Torah scholar.

Goshen — an area of Ancient Egypt in which the Jews lived before the Exodus.

ha'adamah — the blessing recited before eating produce of the ground.

ha'etz — the blessing recited over fruit.

Hashem — God.

Holocaust—term used to describe the systemic murder of European Jewry during World War II.

Israel (as the country)

kavod haTorah — the honor and respect due to the Torah.

Kriyas Yam Suf—the splitting of the Sea of Reeds during the Exodus from Egypt.

mahn — the manna.

makkos — the Ten Plagues in Egypt.

Mashiach — Messiah, the awaited redeemer of Israel, who will usher in an era of universal recognition of the Kingship of Hashem.

matzah — unleavened bread.

Megillas Rus — the Book of Ruth, read on the Festival of Shavuos

Megillas Esther — the Book of Esther, read on the holiday of Purim.

mezonos — the blessing recited before eating grain foods other than bread.

middah (pl. **middos**) — a character trait; an attribute.

mitzvah (pl. **mitzvos**) — a Biblical or Rabbinic commandment; a merit; a good deed.

Moshe Rabbeinu — Moses.

Motza'ei Shabbos — Saturday night; the time of the departure of the Sabbath.

Noach — Noah.

Pesach — Passover.

Purim — the holiday of when Megillas Esther is read.

rebbetzin — (Yiddish) rabbi's wife; also used to refer to a respected Jewish woman.

Seder (pl. **sedarim**) Passove-night ritual during which the Haggadah is recited.

Sefer Bereishis — the Book of Genesis.

Shabbos — the Sabbath.

Shavuos — Festival commemorating the giving of the Torah on Mount Sinai.

shehakol — the blessing recited before eating foods that have no other specific blessing.

Shivah Minim—the seven types of produce for which the Land of Israel is noted; i.e., wheat, barley, grapes, figs, date (honey), olive (oil) and pomegranates.

siyum — celebration marking the completion of a course of Torah or Talmud study.

Succos —the festival during which one dwells in a **succah** and takes the Four Species.

succah — the booth in which Jews are commanded to dwell during the festival of Succos.

tefillah (pl. **tefillos**) — Jewish prayer

Teivah — Noah's Ark.

tzeddakah — charity.

Yom Tov (pl. **Yamim Tovim**) — a Jewish holiday; a Festival

YOUR LIFE.
Hi
love
YOUR BOOK.
צדקה